CONSECRATED PERSONS AND THEIR MISSION IN SCHOOLS

REFLECTIONS AND GUIDELINES

CONGREGATION FOR CATHOLIC EDUCATION

*All booklets are published thanks to the generous support
of the members of the Catholic Truth Society*

CATHOLIC TRUTH SOCIETY
PUBLISHERS TO THE HOLY SEE

CONTENTS

INTRODUCTION

1. The celebration of the two thousandth anniversary of the incarnation of the Word was for many believers a time of conversion and of opening to God's plan for the human person created in his image. The grace of the Jubilee incited in the People of God an urgency to proclaim the mystery of Jesus Christ "yesterday, today and forever" with the testimony of their lives and, in Him, the truth about the human person. Young people, moreover, expressed a surprising interest with regard to the explicit announcement of Jesus. Consecrated persons, for their part, grasped the strong call to live in a state of conversion for accomplishing their specific mission in the Church: to be witnesses of Christ, *epiphany of the love of God in the world,* recognisable signs of reconciled humanity.[1]

At the beginning of the third millennium

2. The complex cultural situations of the beginning of the 21st century are a further appeal to a responsibility to live the present as *kairós*, a favourable time, so that the Gospel may effectively reach the men and women of today. Consecrated persons feel the importance of the prophetic task entrusted to them by the Church in these momentous but fascinating times,[2] *"recalling and serving the divine plan for humanity,* as it is announced in Scripture and as also emerges from the attentive reading of the signs of God's providential action in history."[3] This task requires the courage of testimony and the patience of dialogue; it is a duty before the cultural tendencies that threaten the dignity of human life, especially in the crucial moments of its

a prophetic task

---

[1] Cf. JOHN PAUL II, Apostolic exhortation *Vita consecrata,* 25th March 1996, nn. 72-73, *AAS* 88 (1996), 447-449.
[2] Cf. JOHN PAUL II, Encyclical letter *Redemptoris missio,* 7th December 1990, n. 38, *AAS* 83 (1991), 286.
[3] JOHN PAUL II, Apostolic exhortation *Vita consecrata,* n. 73, *AAS* 88 (1996), 448.

beginning and its ending, the harmony of creation, and the existence of peoples and peace.

the reason for these reflections
3. Within the context of the profound changes that assail the world of education and schools, the Congregation for Catholic Education wishes to share some reflections, offer some guidelines and incite some further investigations of the educational mission and the presence of consecrated persons in schools in general, not only Catholic schools. This document is mainly addressed to members of institutes of consecrated life and of societies of apostolic life, as well as to those who, involved in the educational mission of the Church, have assumed the evangelical counsels in other forms.

as a continuation of previous ecclesial guidelines
4. These considerations are within the lines of the Second Vatican Council, the Magisterium of the universal Church and the documents of the continental Synods regarding evangelisation, the consecrated life and education, especially scholastic education. In recent years, this Congregation has offered guidelines on Catholic schools[4] and on lay people who bear witness to faith in schools.[5] As a continuation of the document on lay people, it now intends reflecting on the specific contribution of consecrated persons to the educational mission in schools in the light of the Apostolic Exhortation *Vita consecrata* and of the more recent developments of pastoral care for culture.[6] This is a result of its conviction that: "a faith that does not become culture is a faith that has not been fully received, not entirely thought through, not loyally lived."[7]

---

[4] Cf. SACRED CONGREGATION FOR CATHOLIC EDUCATION, *The Catholic School,* 19th March 1977; cf. CONGREGATION FOR CATHOLIC EDUCATION, *The Catholic School on the Threshold of the Third Millennium,* 28th December 1997.

[5] Cf. SACRED CONGREGATION FOR CATHOLIC EDUCATION, *Lay Catholics in Schools: Witnesses to Faith,* 15th October 1982.

[6] Cf. PONTIFICAL COUNCIL FOR CULTURE, *Toward a Pastoral Approach to Culture,* 23rd May 1999, *L'Osservatore Romano* (English), N. 23, 9 June 1999.

[7] JOHN PAUL II, *Letter Instituting the Pontifical Council for Culture,* 20th May 1982, *AAS* 74 (1982), 685.

Introduction

5. The necessity for a cultural mediation of the faith is *the cultural* an invitation for consecrated persons to consider the *mediation* meaning of their presence in schools. The altered *of the faith* circumstances in which they operate, in environments *today* that are often laicised and in reduced numbers in educational communities, make it necessary to clearly express their specific contribution in cooperation with the other vocations present in schools. A time emerges in which to process answers to the fundamental questions of the young generations and to present a clear cultural proposal that clarifies the type of person and society to which it is desired to educate, and the reference to the anthropological vision inspired by the values of the gospel, in a respectful and constructive dialogue with the other concepts of life.

6. The challenges of modern life give new motivations *a renewed* to the mission of consecrated persons, called to live *commitment* the evangelic councils and bring the humanism of the *in the* beatitudes to the field of education and schools. This is *educational* not at all foreign to the mandate of the Church to *sphere* announce salvation to all.[8] "At the same time, however, we are painfully aware of certain difficulties which induce your Communities to abandon the school sector. The dearth of religious vocations, estrangement from the teaching apostolate, the attraction of alternative forms of apostolate seemingly more gratifying."[9] Far from discouraging, these difficulties can be a source of purification and characterise a time *of grace and salvation* (cf. *2 Cor* 6:2). They invite discernment and an attitude of constant *renewal*. The Holy Spirit, moreover, guides us to rediscover the charism, the roots and the modalities for our presence

[8] Cf. JOHN PAUL II, Apostolic exhortation *Vita consecrata*, n. 96, *AAS* 88 (1996), 471.
[9] CONGREGATION FOR CATHOLIC EDUCATION, *Circular letter to the Reverend General Superiors and Presidents of Societies of Apostolic Life responsible for Catholic Schools*, 15th October 1996, in *Enchiridion Vaticanum*, vol. 15, 837.

5

in schools, concentrating on the essential: the importance of the testimony of Christ, the poor, humble and chaste one; the priority of the person and of relationships based on love; the search for truth; the synthesis between faith, life and culture and the valid proposal of a view of man that respects God's plan.

Evangelise by educating
It thus becomes clear that consecrated persons in schools, in communion with the Bishops, carry out an ecclesial mission that is vitally important inasmuch as while they educate they are also evangelising. This mission requires a commitment of holiness, generosity and skilled educational professionalism so that the truth about the person as revealed by Jesus may enlighten the growth of the young generations and of the entire community. This Dicastery feels therefore that it is opportune to call attention to the profile of consecrated persons and to reflect on some well-known aspects of their educational mission in schools today.

I. PROFILE OF CONSECRATED PERSONS

At the school of Christ the teacher

7. "The consecrated life, deeply rooted in the example and teaching of Christ the Lord, is a gift of God the Father to his Church through the Holy Spirit. By the profession of the evangelical counsels *the characteristic features of Jesus* - the chaste, poor and obedient one - *are made constantly 'visible' in the midst of the world* and the eyes of the faithful are directed towards the mystery of the Kingdom of God already at work in history, even as it awaits its full realisation in heaven."[10] The aim of the consecrated life is "conformity to the Lord Jesus in *his total self-giving,*"[11] so that every consecrated person is called to assume "his mind and his way of life,"[12] his way of thinking and of acting, of being and of loving.

Ecclesial gift for revealing the Word

8. *The direct reference to Christ and the intimate nature of a gift* for the Church and the world,[13] are elements that define the identity and scope of the consecrated life. In them the consecrated life finds itself, its point of departure, God and his love, and its point of arrival, the human community and its requirements. It is through these elements that every religious family traces its own physiognomy, from its spirituality to its apostolate, from its style of community life to its ascetic plan, to the sharing and participation in the richness of its own charisms.

Identity of consecrated life

---

[10] JOHN PAUL II, Apostolic exhortation *Vita consecrata*, n. 1, *AAS* 88 (1996), 377.
[11] *Ibid.*, n. 65, 441.
[12] *Ibid.*, n. 18, 391.
[13] Cf. SECOND VATICAN ECUMENICAL COUNCIL, Dogmatic Constitution on the Church *Lumen gentium*, nn. 43-44.

At Christ's school to have his mind 9. The consecrated life can be compared in some ways to a *school,* that every consecrated person is called to attend for his whole life. In fact, having the mind of the Son means to attend his school daily, to learn from him to have a heart that is meek and humble, courageous and passionate. It means allowing oneself to be *educated* by Christ, the eternal Word of the Father and, to be drawn to him, the heart and centre of the world, choosing his same *form* of life.

Allowing oneself to be educated and formed by Christ, to be similar to him 10. The life of a consecrated person is therefore an *educational-formative* rise and fall that educates to the truth of life and forms it to the freedom of the gift of oneself, according to the model of the Easter of the Lord. Every moment of consecrated life forms part of this rise and fall, in its double educational and formative aspect. A consecrated person does in fact gradually learn to have the mind of the Son in him and to reveal it in *a life that is increasingly similar to his,* both at individual and community level, in initial and permanent formation. Thus the vows are an expression of the lifestyle chosen by Jesus on this earth that was essential, chaste and completely dedicated to the Father. Prayer becomes a continuation on earth of the praise of the Son to the Father for the salvation of all mankind. Community life is the demonstration that, in the name of the Lord, stronger bonds than those that come from flesh and blood can be tied. These are bonds that are able to overcome what can divide. The apostolate is the impassioned announcement of he by whom we have been conquered.

gift for everyone 11. The school of the mind of the Son gradually opens the consecrated life to the urgency for testimony, so that *the gift may reach everyone.* In fact, Christ "did not count equality with God a thing to be grasped" (*Phil* 2:6), he kept nothing for himself, but shared his

8

wealth of being Son with all men. That is why, even when the testimony contests some elements of the local culture, consecrated persons try to enter into a dialogue in order to share the wealth which they bring. This means that the testimony must be distinct and unequivocal, clear and comprehensible for everyone, in order to demonstrate that religious consecration has much to say to every culture inasmuch as it helps to reveal the truth about human beings.

Radical response

12. Among the challenges that the consecrated life faces today is that of trying to demonstrate the *anthropological value* of consecration. It is a question of demonstrating that a poor, chaste and obedient life enhances intimate human dignity; that *everyone* is called, in a different way, according to his or her vocation, to be poor, obedient and chaste. The evangelical counsels do, in fact, transfigure authentically human values and desires, but they also relativise the human "by pointing to God as the absolute good."[14] The consecrated life, moreover, must be able to show that the evangelical message possesses considerable importance for living in today's world and is also comprehensible for those who live in a competitive society such as ours. Lastly, the consecrated life must try to testify that holiness is the highest humanising proposal of man and of history; it is a project that everyone on earth can make his or her own.[15]

Anthropological value of the consecrated life

13. Consecrated persons communicate the richness of their specific vocation to the extent that they live their consecration commitments to the full. On the other hand, such a communication also arouses in the receiver a

---

[14] JOHN PAUL II, Apostolic exhortation *Vita consecrata*, n. 87, *AAS* 88 (1996), 463.
[15] Cf. JOHN PAUL II, Apostolic letter *Novo millennio ineunte,* 6th January 2001, n.30, *AAS* 93 (2001), 287.

capacity for an enriching response through the participation of his personal gift and his specific vocation. This "confrontation-sharing" with the Church and with the world is of great importance for the vitality of the *Charismatic* various religious charisms and for their interpretation in *circularity* line with the modern context and their respective spiritual roots. It is the principle of *charismatic circularity*, as a result of which the charism *returns* in a sort of way to where it was born, but without simply repeating itself. In this way, the consecrated life itself is renewed, in the listening and interpretation of the signs of the times and in the creative and active fidelity of its origins.

Constructive 14.The validity of this principle is confirmed by history; *dialogue in* the consecrated life has always woven a constructive *the past* dialogue with local culture, sometimes questioning and *and in the* provoking it, at others defending and preserving it, but in *present* any case allowing it to stimulate and interrogate, in a confrontation that was in some cases dialectic, but always fruitful. It is important that such a confrontation continues even in these times of renewal for the consecrated life and of cultural disorientation that risks frustrating the human heart's insuppressible need for truth.

In the Church communion

The Church 15. The study of the ecclesial situation as a mystery of *mystery of* communion has led the Church, under the action of the *communion* Spirit, to increasingly understand itself as the pilgrim people of God and, at the same time as the body of Christ the members of which are in a mutual relationship with each other and with the head.

At a pastoral level, "to make the Church *the home and the school of communion*"[16] is the great challenge that we must know how to face, at the beginning of the new

---

[16] *Ibid.*, n. 43, 296.

millennium, in order to be faithful to God's plan and to the world's deep expectations. It is first and foremost necessary to promote a *spirituality of communion* capable of becoming the educational principle in the various environments in which the human person is formed. This *spirituality* is learned by making our hearts ponder on the mystery of the Trinity, whose light is reflected in the face of every person, and welcomed and appreciated as a gift.

16. Demands for communion have offered consecrated persons the chance to rediscover the mutual relationship with the other vocations in the people of God. In the Church they are called, in a special way, to reveal that participation in the Trinitarian communion can change human relations creating a new kind of solidarity. By professing to live *for God and of God,* consecrated persons do, in fact, undertake to preach the power of the peacemaking action of grace that overcomes the disruptive dynamisms present in the human heart.

Consecrated persons in the Church-communion

17. Whatever the specific charism that characterises them, consecrated persons are called, through their vocations, to be *experts of communion,* to promote human and spiritual bonds that promote the mutual exchange of gifts between all the members of the people of God. The acknowledgement of the *many forms* of vocations in the Church gives a new meaning to the presence of consecrated persons in the field of scholastic education. For them a school is a place of mission, where the prophetic role conferred by baptism and lived according to the requirements of the radicalism typical of the evangelical counsels is fulfilled. The gift of special consecration that they have received will lead them to recognising in schools and in the educational commitment the fruitful furrow in which the Kingdom of God can grow and bear fruit.

with the dynamism of the specific charism

A conse-crated person educates... 18. This commitment responds perfectly to the nature and to the scope of the consecrated life itself and is carried out according to that double *educational and formative* model that accompanies the growth of the individual consecrated person. Through schools, men and women religious educate, help young people to grasp their own identity and to reveal those authentic needs and desires that inhabit everyone's heart, but which often remain unknown and underestimated: thirst for authenticity and honesty, for love and fidelity, for truth and consistency, for happiness and fullness of life. Desires which in the final analysis converge in the supreme human desire: *to see the face of God.*

... forms 19. The second modality is that regarding formation. A school *forms* when it offers a precise proposal for fulfilling those desires, preventing them from being deformed, or only partially or weakly achieved. With the testimony of their lives consecrated persons, who are at the school of the Lord, propose that form of existence which is inspired by Christ, so that even a young person may live the freedom of being a child of God and may experiment the true joy and authentic fulfilment that spring from the project of the Father. Consecrated persons have a providential mission in schools, in the modern context, where the educational proposals seem to be increasingly poorer and man's aspirations seem to be increasingly unanswered!

in schools, educational communities 20. There is no need for consecrated persons to reserve exclusive tasks for themselves in educational communities. The specificity of the consecrated life lies in its being a sign, a memory and prophecy of the values of the Gospel. Its characteristic is "to bring to bear on the world of education their radical witness to the values of the Kingdom,"[17] in cooperation with the laity called to express, in the sign of secularity, the realism of the Incarnation of God in our midst, "the intimate dependency of earthly situations on God in Christ."[18]

21. The different vocations operate for the growth of the body of Christ and of his mission in the world. The commitment to evangelical testimony according to the typical form of every vocation gives rise to a dynamism of mutual help to fully live membership of the mystery of Christ and of the Church in its many dimensions; a stimulus for each one to discover the evangelical richness of his or her own vocation in a gratitude-filled comparison with others.

by developing the specificity of all the vocations present in the educational community

By avoiding both confrontation and homologation, the reciprocity of vocations seems to be a particularly fertile prospect for enriching the ecclesial value of educational communities. In them the various vocations carry out a service for achieving a culture of communion. They are correlative, different and mutual paths that converge to bring to fulfillment the charism of charisms: love.

Before the world

22. The awareness that they are living in a time that is full of challenges and new possibilities urges consecrated persons, involved in the educational mission in schools, to make good use of the gift received by accounting for the hope that animates them. Fruit of the faith in the God of history, hope is based on the word and on the life of Jesus, who lived *in the world,* without being *of the world.* He asks the same attitude from those who follow him: to live and work in history, without however allowing oneself to

Accounting for hope

---

[17] JOHN PAUL II, Apostolic exhortation *Vita consecrata*, n. 96, *AAS* 88 (1996), 472.
[18] SACRED CONGREGATION FOR CATHOLIC EDUCATION, *Lay Catholics in Schools: Witnesses to Faith*, n. 43.

be imprisoned by it. Hope demands insertion in the world, but also separation; it requires prophecy and sometimes involves following or withdrawing in order to educate the children of God to freedom in a context of influences that lead to new forms of slavery.

Discernment and contemplative gaze 23. This way of being in history requires a deep capacity for discernment. Born from daily listening to the Word of God, this facilitates the interpreting events and prepares for becoming, as if to say, a *critical conscience*. The deeper and more authentic this commitment, the more likely it will be to grasp the action of the Spirit in the life of people and in the events of history. Such a capacity finds its foundation in contemplation and in prayer, which teach us to see persons and things from God's viewpoint. This is the contrary of a superficial glance and of an activism that is incapable of reflecting on the important and the essential. When there is no contemplation and prayer - and consecrated persons are not exempt from this risk - passion for the announcement of the Gospel is also lacking as is the capacity to fight for the life and salvation of mankind.

In schools for educating to silence and to meeting God 24. By living their vocations with generosity and eagerness, consecrated persons bring to schools their experience of a relationship with God, based on prayer, the Eucharist, the sacrament of Reconciliation and the spirituality of communion that characterises the life of religious communities. The evangelical position that results facilitates discernment and the formation of a critical sense, a fundamental and necessary aspect of the educational process. Whatever their specific task, the presence of consecrated persons in schools *infects* the contemplative glance by educating to a silence that leads to listening to God, to paying attention to others,

14

to the situation that surrounds us, to creation. Furthermore, by aiming at the essential, consecrated persons provoke the need for authentic encounters, they renew the capacity to be amazed and to take care of the other, rediscovered like a brother.

25. Because of their role, consecrated persons are "*a living memorial of Jesus' way of living and acting* as the Incarnate Word in relation to the Father and in relation to the brethren.*"*[19] The first and fundamental contribution to the educational mission in schools by consecrated persons is the evangelical completeness of their lives. This way of shaping their lives, based on their generous response to God's call, becomes an invitation to all the members of the educational community to make their lives a response to God, according to their various states of life.

for living the Gospel to the full

26. In this perspective, consecrated persons testify that the *chastity* of their hearts, bodies, lives is the full and strong expression of a total love for God that renders a person free, full of deep joy and ready for their mission. Thus consecrated persons contribute to guiding young men and women towards the full development of their capacity to love and a complete maturation of their personalities. This is a very important testimony in a culture that increasingly tends to trivialise human love and close itself to life. In a society where everything tends to be free, consecrated persons, through their freely chosen *poverty,* take on a simple and essential lifestyle, promoting a correct relationship with things and trusting in Divine Providence. Freedom from things makes them unreservedly ready for an educational service to the young that becomes a sign of the availability of God's love in a world where

and testifying a chaste, poor and obedient life

---

[19] JOHN PAUL II, Apostolic exhortation *Vita consecrata*, n. 22, *AAS* 88 (1996), 396.

materialism and having seem to prevail over being. Finally, by living *obedience,* they remind everyone of the lordship of the only God and, against the temptation of dominion, they indicate a choice of faith that counters forms of individualism and self-sufficiency.

*and
expressing
their
donation*

27. Just as Jesus did for his disciples, so consecrated persons live their donation for the benefit of the receivers of their mission: students, in the first place, but also their parents and other educators. This encourages them to live prayer and their daily response to their following Christ to become an increasingly more suitable instrument for the work that God achieves through them.

The call to give themselves fully to schools, in deep and true freedom, means that consecrated men and women become a living testimony to the Lord who offers himself for everyone. This excess of gratuitousness and love makes their donation assessable over and above any type of usefulness.[20]

*looking at
Mary*

28. Consecrated persons find in Mary the model to inspire them in their relations with God and in living human history. Mary is the icon of prophetic hope because of her capacity to welcome and meditate at length on the Word in her heart, of interpreting history according to God's plan, of contemplating God present and working in time. In her eyes we see the wisdom that unites in harmony the ecstasy of her meeting with God and the greatest critical realism with regard to the world. The *Magnificat* is the prophecy *par excellence* of the Virgin. It always sounds new in the spirit of a consecrated person, as a constant praise to the Lord who bends down to the least and to the poor to give them life and mercy.

[20] Cf. *Ibid.,* n. 105, 481.

II THE EDUCATIONAL MISSION OF CONSECRATED PERSONS TODAY

29. A profile of consecrated persons clearly shows how their educational commitment in schools is suited to the nature of the consecrated life. In fact "thanks to their experience of the particular gifts of the Spirit, their careful listening to the Word, their constant practice of discernment and their rich heritage of pedagogical traditions amassed since the establishment of their Institutes...consecrated persons give life to educational undertakings"[21] in the educational field. This requires the promotion within the consecrated life, on the one hand, of a "renewed cultural commitment which seeks to raise the level of personal preparation,[22] and on the other of a constant conversion to follow Jesus, *the way, the truth and the life* (cf. *Jn* 14:6). It is an uncomfortable and tiring road that does however make it possible to take up the challenges of the present time and undertake the educational mission entrusted to the Church. While aware that it cannot be exhaustive, the Congregation for Catholic Education, intends pausing to consider just some elements of this mission. In particular it wishes to reflect on three specific contributions of the presence of consecrated persons to scholastic education: first of all the link of education to evangelisation; then formation to "vertical" relationism, that is to the opening to God and lastly formation to "horizontal" relationism, that is to say to welcoming the other and to living together.

---

[21] CONGREGATION FOR INSTITUTES OF CONSECRATED LIFE AND SOCIETIES OF APOSTOLIC LIFE, *Starting Afresh from Christ,* 19th May 2002, n. 39.
[22] *Ibid.,* n. 39.

Educators called to evangelise

Go...preach the Gospel to the whole creation (Mk 16:15)

The educational experience of consecrated persons

30. "To fulfil the mandate she has received from her divine founder of proclaiming the mystery of salvation to all men and of restoring all things in Christ, Holy Mother the Church must be concerned with the whole of men's life, even the secular part of it insofar as it has a bearing on his heavenly calling."[23] Both in Catholic and in other types of schools, the educational commitment for consecrated persons is a vocation and choice of life, a path to holiness, a demand for justice and solidarity especially towards the poorest young people, threatened by various forms of deviancy and risk. By devoting themselves to the educational mission in schools, consecrated persons contribute to making the bread of culture reach those in most need of it. They see in culture a fundamental condition for people to completely fulfil themselves, achieve a level of life that conforms to their dignity and open themselves to encounter with Christ and the Gospel. Such a commitment is founded on a patrimony of pedagogical wisdom that makes it possible to confirm the value of education as a force that is able to help the maturing of a person, to draw him to the faith and to respond to the challenges of such a complex society as that which we have today.

Faced with modern challenges

The global-isation process

31. The process of globalisation characterises the horizon of the new century. This is a complex phenomenon in its dynamics. It has positive effects, such as the possibility for peoples and cultures to meet,

---

[23] SECOND VATICAN ECUMENICAL COUNCIL, Declaration on Christian Education *Gravissimum educationis*, Introd.

but also negative aspects, which risk producing further disparities, injustices and marginalisation. The rapidity and complexity of the changes produced by globalisation are also reflected in schools, which risk being exploited by the demands of the productive-economic structures, or by ideological prejudices and political calculations that obscure their educational function. This situation incites schools to strongly reassert their specific role of stimulus to reflection and critical aspiration. Because of their vocation consecrated persons undertake to promote the dignity of the human person, cooperating with schools so that they may become places of overall education, evangelisation and learning of a vital dialogue between persons of different cultures, religions and social backgrounds.[24]

32. The growing development and diffusion of new *new* technologies provide means and instruments that were *technologies* unconceivable up to just a few years ago. However, they also give rise to questions concerning the future of human development. The vastness and depth of technological innovations influence the processes of access to knowledge, socialisation, relations with nature and they foreshadow radical, not always positive, changes in huge sectors of the life of mankind. Consecrated persons cannot shirk wondering about the impact that these technologies will have on people, on means of communication, on the future of society.

33. Within the context of these changes, schools have *schools'* a meaningful role to play in the formation of the *task* personalities of the new generations. The responsible use of the new technologies, especially of internet,

---

[24] Cf. CONGREGATION FOR CATHOLIC EDUCATION, *The Catholic School on the Threshold of the Third Millennium*, n. 11.

demands an appropriate ethical formation.[25] Together with those working in schools, consecrated persons feel the need to understand the processes, languages, opportunities and challenges of the new technologies, but above all to become *communication educators,* so that these technologies may be used with discernment and wisdom.[26]

...for the future of man

34. Among the challenges of modern society that schools have to face are threats to life and to families, genetic manipulations, growing pollution, plundering of natural resources, the unsolved drama of the underdevelopment and poverty that crush entire populations of the south of the world. These are vital questions for everyone, which need to be faced with extensive and responsible vision, promoting a concept of life that respects the dignity of man and of creation. This means forming persons who are able to dominate and transform processes and instruments in a sense that is humanising and filled with solidarity. This concern is shared by the whole international community, that is active in assuring that national educational programmes contribute to developing training initiatives in this regard.[27]

An explicit anthropological view

Necessity for an anthropo- logical foundation

35. The clarification of the anthropological foundation of the formative proposal of schools is an increasingly more unavoidable urgency in our complex societies.

The human person is defined by his *rationality,* that is by his intelligent and free nature, and by his *relational*

---

[25] Cf. PONTIFICAL COUNCIL FOR SOCIAL COMMUNICATIONS, *Ethics in Internet,* 22nd February 2002, n. 15.
[26] Cf. PONTIFICAL COUNCIL FOR SOCIAL COMMUNICATIONS *The Church and Internet,* 22nd February 2002, n. 7.
[27] Cf. UNESCO, CONFERENCE GENERALE, *Résolution adoptée sur le rapport de la Commission V. Séance plénière,* 12 november 1997.

nature, that is by his relationship with other persons. Living with others involves both the level of the being of the human person - man/woman - and the ethical level of his acting. The foundation of human *ethos* is in being the image and likeness of God, the Trinity of persons in communion. The existence of a person appears therefore as a call to the duty to exist for one another.

36. The commitment of a spirituality of communion for the 21st century is the expression of a concept of the human person, created in the image of God. This view enlightens the mystery of man and woman. The human person experiences his humanity to the extent that he is able to participate in the humanity of the other, the bearer of a unique and unrepeatable plan. This is a plan that can only be carried out within the context of the relation and dialogue with the *you* in a dimension of reciprocity and opening to God. This kind of reciprocity is at the basis of the gift of self and of *closeness* as an opening in solidarity with every other person. This closeness has its truest root in the mystery of Christ, the Word Incarnate, who wished to become close to man.

37. Faced with ideological pluralism and the proliferation of "knowledge", consecrated men and women therefore offer the contribution of a vision of a *plenary humanism,*[28] open to God, who loves everyone and invites them to become increasingly more "conformed to the image of his Son" (cf. *Rm* 8:29). This divine plan is the heart of Christian humanism: "Christ...fully reveals man to man himself and makes his supreme calling clear."[29] To confirm the greatness of the human creature does not mean to ignore his

within the dimension of a plenary humanism

---

[28] Cf. PAUL VI, Encyclical letter *Populorum progressio,* 26th March 1967, n. 42, *AAS* 59 (1967), 278.
[29] SECOND VATICAN ECUMENICAL COUNCIL, Pastoral Constitution on the Church in the Modern World *Gaudium et spes,* n. 22.

fragility: the image of God reflected in persons is in fact deformed by sin. The illusion of freeing oneself from all dependency, even from God, always ends up in new forms of slavery, violence and suppression. This is confirmed by the experience of each human being, by the history of blood shed in the name of ideologies and regimes that wished to construct a *new humanity* without God.[30] On the contrary, in order to be authentic, freedom must measure itself according to the truth of the person, the fullness of which is revealed in Christ, and lead to a liberation from all that denies his dignity preventing him from achieving his own good and that of others.

Witnesses of the truth about the human person

38. Consecrated persons undertake to be witnesses in schools to the truth about persons and to the transforming power of the Holy Spirit. With their lives they confirm that faith enlightens the whole field of education by raising and strengthening human values. Catholic schools especially have a priority: that of "bringing forth within what is learnt in school a Christian vision of the world, of life, of culture and of history."[31]

with cultural mediation

39. Hence the importance of reasserting, in a pedagogical context that tends to put it in the background, the humanistic and spiritual dimension of knowledge and of the various school subjects. Through study and research a person contributes to perfecting himself and his humanity. Study becomes the path for a personal encounter with the truth, a "place" of encounter with God himself. Taken this way, knowledge can help to motivate existence, to begin the search for God, it can be a great experience

---

[30] Cf. JOHN PAUL II, Encyclical letter *Redemptoris missio*, n. 8, *AAS* 83 (1991), 256.
[31] CONGREGATION FOR CATHOLIC EDUCATION, *The Catholic School on the Threshold of the Third Millennium*, n. 14.

of freedom for truth, placing itself in the service of the maturation and promotion of humanity.[32] Such a commitment demands of consecrated persons an accurate analysis of the quality of their educational proposal, and also constant attention to their cultural and *professional* formation.

40. Another, equally important, field of evangelisation and humanisation is non-formal education, that is of those who have been unable to have access to normal schooling. Consecrated persons feel that they should be present and promote innovative projects in such contexts. In these situations poorer young people should be given the chance of a suitable formation that considers their moral, spiritual and religious development and is able to promote socialisation and overcome discrimination. This is no novelty, inasmuch as working classes have always been within the sphere of various religious families. It is a case of confirming today with suitable means and plans an attention that has never been lacking.

and commitment in the field of non-formal education

Educators called to accompany towards the Other

We wish to see Jesus (Jn 12:21)

The dynamism of reciprocity

41. The educational mission is carried out in a spirit of cooperation between various subjects - students, parents, teachers, non-teaching personnel and the school management - who form the educational community. It can create an environment for living in which the values are mediated by authentic interpersonal relations

In the educational community

---

[32] Cf. JOHN PAUL II, *Speech to the Plenary Session of the Pontifical Academy of Sciences,* 13th November 2000, *AAS* 93 (2001), 202-206.

between the various members of which it is composed. Its highest aim is the complete and comprehensive education of the person. In this respect, consecrated persons can offer a decisive contribution, in the light of their experience of communion that characterises their community lives. In fact, by committing themselves to live and communicate the spirituality of communion in the school community, through a dialogue that is constructive and able to harmonise differences, they build an environment that is rooted in the evangelical values of truth and love. Consecrated persons are thus leaven that is able to create relations of increasingly deep communion, that are in themselves educational. They promote solidarity, mutual enhancement and joint responsibility in the educational plan, and, above all, they give an explicit Christian testimony, through communication of the experience of God and of the evangelical message, even sharing the awareness of being instruments of God and bearers of a charism in the service of all men.

within the sphere of the Church communion 42. The task of communicating the spirituality of communion within the school community derives from being part of the Church communion. This means that consecrated persons involved in the educational mission must be integrated, starting from their charism, in the pastoral activity of the local Church. They, in fact, carry out an ecclesial ministry in the service of a concrete community and in communion with the Diocesan Ordinary. The common educational mission entrusted to them by the Church does, however, require cooperation and greater synergy between the various religious families. Apart from offering a more skilled educational service, this synergy offers the chance for sharing charisms from which the entire Church will gain. For this reason the communion that consecrated persons are called to experiment goes well beyond their own religious family or institute. Indeed, by opening themselves to communion with other forms of consecration, consecrated persons can "rediscover their common Gospel roots and together grasp the beauty of their own identity in the variety of charisms with greater clarity."[33]

The relational dimension

43. The educational community expresses the variety and beauty of the various vocations and the fruitfulness at educational and pedagogical level that this contributes to the life of scholastic institutions. The commitment to promote the relational dimension of the person and the care taken in establishing authentic educational relationships with young people are undoubtedly aspects that the presence of consecrated persons can facilitate in schools, considered as microcosms in which oases are created where the bases are laid for living responsibly in the macrocosm of society. It is not, however, strange to observe, even in schools, the progressive deterioration of interpersonal relations, due to the functionalisation of roles, haste, fatigue and other factors that create conflicting situations. To organise schools like gymnasiums where one exercises to establish positive relationships between the various members and to search for peaceful solutions to the conflicts is a fundamental objective not just for the life of the educational community, but also for the construction of a society of peace and harmony.

promoting authentic relations

44. Usually in schools there are boys and girls, as well as men and women with tasks of teaching or administration. Consideration of the single-dual

educating to reciprocity

---

[33] CONGREGATION FOR INSTITUTES OF CONSECRATED LIFE AND SOCIETIES OF APOSTOLIC LIFE, *Starting Afresh from Christ*, n. 30.

dimension of the human person implies the need to educate to mutual acknowledgement, in respect and acceptance of differences. The experience of man/woman reciprocity may appear paradigmatic in the positive management of other differences, including ethnic and religious ones. It does, in fact, develop and encourage positive attitudes, such as an awareness that every person can give and receive, a willingness to welcome the other, a capacity for a serene dialogue and a chance to purify and clarify one's own experience while seeking to communicate it and compare it with the other.

through enhancing relations 45. In a relationship of reciprocity, interaction can be asymmetric from the point of view of roles, as it is necessarily in the educational relationship, but not from that of the dignity and uniqueness of every human person. Learning is facilitated when, without undue straining with regard to roles, educational interaction is at a level that fully recognises the equality of the dignity of every human person. In this way it is possible to form personalities capable of having their own view of life and to agree with their choice. The involvement of families and teaching staff creates a climate of trust and respect that promotes the development of the capacity for dialogue and peaceful coexistence in the search for whatever favours the common good.

The educational community

creating an educational environment 46. Due to their experience of community life, consecrated persons are in a most favourable position for cooperating to make the educational plan of the school promote the creation of a true community. In particular they propose an alternative model of coexistence to that of a standardised or individualistic society. In actual fact consecrated persons undertake, together with their lay

26

colleagues, to assure that schools are structured as places of encounter, listening, communication, where students experience values in an essential way. They help, in a directed way, to guide pedagogical choices to promote overcoming individualistic self-promotion, solidarity instead of competition, assisting the weak instead of marginalisation, responsible participation instead of indifference.

47. The family comes first in being responsible for the education of its children. Consecrated persons appreciate the presence of parents in the educational community and try to establish a true relation of reciprocity with them. Participating bodies, personal meetings and other initiatives are aimed at rendering increasingly more active the insertion of parents in the life of institutions and for making them aware of the educational task. Acknowledgement of this task is more necessary today than it was in the past, due to the many difficulties that families now experience. When God's original plan for families is overshadowed in peoples' minds, society receives incalculable damage and the right of children to live in an environment of fully human love is infringed. On the contrary, when a family reflects God's plan, it becomes a workshop where love and true solidarity are experienced.[34]

aware of the family's task

Consecrated persons announce this truth, which does not regard just believers, but is the patrimony of all mankind, inscribed in the heart of man. The chance of contact with the families of the children and young people is a favourable occasion for examining with them meaningful questions regarding life, human love and the nature of families and for agreeing to the proposed vision instead of other often dominating visions.

---

[34] Cf. JOHN PAUL II, *Homily for the Jubilee of Families*, Rome, 15th October 2000, nn. 4-5, *AAS* 93 (2001), 90.

and of the
importance
of brother-
hood as a
prophetic
sign

48. By testifying to Christ and living their typical life of communion, consecrated men and women offer the whole educational community the prophetic sign of brotherhood. Community life, when woven with deep relationships "is itself *prophetic* in a society which, sometimes without realising it, has a profound yearning for a brotherhood which knows no borders."[35] This conviction becomes visible in the commitment to make the life of the community a place of growth of persons and of mutual aid in the search and fulfilment of the common mission. In this regard it is important that the sign of brotherhood can be perceived with transparency in every moment of the life of the scholastic community.

in network
with other
educational
agencies

49. The educational community achieves its scopes in synergy with other educational institutions present in the country.

By coordinating with other educational agencies and in the more extensive communications network a school stimulates the process of personal, professional and social growth of its students, by offering a number of proposals in integrated form. Above all, it forms a most important aid for escaping various conditionings, especially of the *media,* so helping young people to pass from simple and passive consumers to critical interlocutors, capable of positively influencing public opinion and even the quality of information.

Going towards the Other

A lifestyle
that
questions

50. When involved in the serious search for truth through the contribution of the different subjects, the life of the educational community is constantly urged to mature in reflection, to go beyond the acquisitions achieved and to question at the existential level.

---

[35] JOHN PAUL II, Apostolic exhortation *Vita consecrata*, n. 85, *AAS* 88 (1996), 462.

With their presence, consecrated persons offer in this context the specific contribution of their identity and vocation. Even if not always consciously, young people wish to find in them the testimony of a life lived as the answer to a call, as a journey towards God, as the search for the signs through which He makes himself present. They expect to see persons who invite them to seriously question themselves, and to discover the deepest meaning of human existence and of history.

Guide in a search for meaning

51. An encounter with God is always a personal event, an answer that is by its nature, a person's free act in response to the gift of faith. Schools, even Catholic schools, do not demand adherence to the faith, however, they can prepare for it. Through the educational plan it is possible to create the conditions for a person to develop a gift for searching and to be guided in discovering the mystery of his being and of the reality that surrounds him, until he reaches the threshold of the faith. *develop the gift for searching*

To those who then decide to cross this threshold the necessary means are offered for continuing to deepen their experience of faith through prayer, the sacraments, the encounter with Christ in the Word, in the Eucharist, in events and persons.[36]

52. An essential dimension of the path of searching is education to freedom, typical of every school loyal to its task. Education to freedom is a humanising action, because it aims at the full development of personality. In fact, education itself must be seen as the acquisition, growth and possession of freedom. It is a matter of educating each student to free him/herself from the conditionings that prevent him/her from fully *educating to freedom*

[36] Cf. CONGREGATION FOR CATHOLIC EDUCATION, *The Religious Dimension of Education in a Catholic School*, 7th April 1988, nn. 98-112.

living as a person, to form him/herself into a strong and responsible personality, capable of making free and consistent choices.[37]

preparing the ground for the choice of faith
Educating truly free people is in itself already guiding them to the faith. The search for meaning favours the development of the religious dimension of a person as ground in which the Christian choice can mature and the gift of faith can develop. It is ever more frequently observed that in schools, especially in western societies, the religious dimension of a person has become a *lost link,* not only in the typically educational sphere of schools, but also in the more extensive formative process that began in the family.

Yet, without it the formative process, as a whole, is strongly affected, making any search for God difficult. The immediate, the superficial, the accessory, prefabricated solutions, deviations towards magic and surrogates of mystery thus tend to grasp the interest of young people and leave no room for opening to the transcendent.

Even teachers, who call themselves non-believers, today feel the urgency to recover the religious dimension of education, necessary for forming personalities able to manage the powerful conditionings under way in society and to ethically guide the new discoveries of science and technology.

with a style of interpellant education
53. By living the evangelical counsels, consecrated persons form an effective invitation to question themselves about God and the mystery of life. Such a question that requires a style of education that is able to stimulate fundamental questions on the origin and meaning of life passes through the search for the *whys* more than for the *hows*. For this reason, it is necessary to check how the contents of the various subjects are

---

[37] Cf. SACRED CONGREGATION FOR CATHOLIC EDUCATION, *The Catholic School,* n. 31.

proposed in order that students may develop such questions and search for suitable replies. Moreover, children and young people should be encouraged to flee from the obvious and from the trivial, especially within the sphere of choices of life, of the family, of human love. This style is translated into a methodology of study and research that trains for reflection and discernment. It takes the form of a strategy that cultivates in the person, from his earliest years, an inner life as the place to listen to the voice of God, cultivate the meaning of the sacred, decide to follow values, mature the recognition of one's limits and of sin, feel the growth of the responsibility for every human being.

Teaching religion

54. The teaching of religion assumes a specific role in this context. Consecrated persons, together with other educators, but with a greater responsibility, are often called to ensure specialised paths of religious education, depending on the different school situations: in some schools the majority of the pupils are Christians, in others different religious followings predominate, or there are agnostic or atheist choices. Their's is the duty to emphasise the value of the teaching of religion within the timetable of the institution and within the cultural programme. Even while acknowledging that the teaching of religion in a Catholic school has a different function from that which it has in other schools, its scope is still that of opening to the understanding of the historical experience of Christianity, of guiding to knowledge of Jesus Christ and the study of his Gospel. In this sense, it can be described as a cultural proposal that can be offered to everyone over and above their personal choices of faith. In many contexts, Christianity already forms the spiritual *horizon* of the native culture.

Specialised religious education itineraries

cultural proposal offered to everyone

31

teaching of religion in Catholic schools In Catholic schools, teaching of religion must help students to arrive at a personal position in religious matters that is consistent and respectful of the positions of others, so contributing to their growth and to a more complete understanding of reality. It is important that the whole educational community, especially in Catholic schools, recognises the value and role of the teaching of religion and contributes to its enhancement by the students. By using words that are suited to mediating the religious message, the religion teacher is called to stimulate the pupils to study the great questions concerning the meaning of life, the significance of reality and a responsible commitment to transform it in the light of the evangelical values and modern culture.

other formative opportunities The community of a Catholic school offers not only teaching of religion but also other opportunities, other moments and ways for educating to a harmony between faith and culture, faith and life.[38]

Life as a vocation

Life as a gift and as a task 55. Together with other Christian educators, consecrated persons know how to grasp and enhance the vocational dimension that is intrinsic to the educational process. Life is, in fact, a gift that is accomplished in the free response to a special call, to be discovered in the concrete circumstances of each day. Care for the vocational dimension guides the person to interpret his existence in the light of God's plan.

The absence or scarce attention to the vocational dimension not only deprives young people of the assistance to which they have a right in the important discernment on the fundamental choices of their lives, but it also impoverishes society and the Church, both

---

[38] Cf. *Ibid.*, nn. 37-48.

of which are in need of the presence of people able to devote themselves on a stable basis to the service of God, their brothers and the common good.

Culture of vocations

56. The promotion of a *new* vocational culture is a fundamental component of the new evangelisation. Through it, one must "find courage and zest for the big questions, those related to one's future."[39] These are questions that should be reawakened even through personalised educational processes by means of which one is gradually led to discover life as a gift of God and as a task. These processes can form a real itinerary of vocational maturation, that leads to a specific vocation. *Re-awakening a taste for the big questions*

Consecrated persons especially are called to promote the *culture of vocations* in schools. They are a sign for all Christian people not only of a specific vocation, but also of vocational dynamism as a form of life, thus eloquently representing the decision of those who wish to live with attention to God's call.

57. In the modern situation, the educational mission in schools is increasingly shared with the laity. "Whereas at times in the recent past, collaboration came about as a means of supplementing the decline of consecrated persons necessary to carry out activities, now it is growing out of the need to share responsibility not only in the carrying out of the Institute's works but especially in the hope of sharing specific aspects and moments of the spirituality and mission of the Institute."[40] Consecrated persons must therefore transmit the educational charism that animates them and promote *sharing their educational charism*

---

[39] PONTIFICAL WORK FOR ECCLESIASTICAL VOCATIONS, *New Vocations for a New Europe*. Final document of the Congress of Vocations to the Priesthood and to Consecrated life, Rome, 5th -10th May 1997, n.13 b.
[40] CONGREGATION FOR INSTITUTES OF CONSECRATED LIFE AND SOCIETIES OF APOSTOLIC LIFE, *Starting Afresh from Christ,* n. 31.

the formation of those who feel that they are called to the same mission. To discharge this responsibility they must be careful not to get involved exclusively in academic-administrative tasks and to not be taken over by activism. What they must do is favour attention to the richness of their charism and try to develop it in response to the new social-cultural situations.

becoming privileged interlocutors in the search for God

58. In educational communities consecrated persons can promote the achievement of a mentality that is inspired by the evangelical values in a style that is typical of their charism. This in itself is already an educational service in a vocational key. Young people, in fact, and often also the other members of the educational community, more or less consciously expect to find in consecrated persons privileged interlocutors in the search for God. For this type of service, the most specific of the identity of consecrated persons, there are no age limits that would justify considering oneself retired. Even when they have to retire from professional activity, they can always continue to be available for young people and adults, as experts of life according to the Spirit, men and women educators in the sphere of faith.

The presence of consecrated men and women in schools is thus a proposal of evangelical spirituality, a reference point for the members of the educational community in their itinerary of faith and of Christian maturation.

The vocational dimension of the teaching profession

59. The quality of the teachers is fundamental in creating an educational environment that is purposeful and fertile. It is for this reason that the institutions of consecrated life and religious communities, especially when in charge of Catholic schools, propose formation itineraries for teachers. It is opportune in these to

34

emphasise the vocational dimension of the teaching profession in order to make the teachers aware that they are participating in the educational and sanctifying mission of the Church.[41] Consecrated persons can reveal, to those who so desire, the richness of the spirituality that characterises them and of the charism of their Institute, encouraging them to live them in the educational ministry according to the lay identity and in forms that are suitable and accessible to young people.

Educators called to teach coexistence

....all men will know that you are my disciples,
if you have love for one another (Jn 13:35)

On a human scale

60. A school's community dimension is inseparable from priority attention to the person, the focus of the scholastic educational programme. *"Culture must correspond to the human person,* and overcome the temptation to a knowledge which yields to pragmatism or which loses itself in the endless meanderings of erudition. Such knowledge is incapable of giving meaning to life...knowledge enlightened by faith, far from abandoning areas of daily life, invests them with all the strength of hope and prophecy. The humanism which we desire advocates a vision of society centred on the human person and his inalienable rights, on the values of justice and peace, on a correct relationship between individuals, society and the State, on the logic of solidarity and subsidiarity. It is a humanism capable of giving a soul to economic progress itself, so that it may be directed to the *promotion of each individual and of the whole person."*[42]

Priority attention to the person

---

[41] Cf. SACRED CONGREGATION FOR CATHOLIC EDUCATION, *Lay Catholics in Schools: Witnesses to Faith,* n. 24.

[42] JOHN PAUL II, *Jubilee of University Professors,* Rome, 9th September 2000, nn. 3, 6, *AAS* 92 (2000), 863-865.

*character-
ising
concrete
choices in
that sense*

61. Consecrated persons must be careful to safeguard the priority of the person in their educational programme. For this they must cooperate in the concrete choices that are made regarding the general school programme and its formative proposal. Each pupil must be considered as an individual, bearing in mind his family environment, his personal history, his skills and his interests. In a climate of mutual trust, consecrated men and women discover and cultivate each person's talents and help young people to become responsible for their own formation and to cooperate in that of their companions. This requires the total dedication and unselfishness of those who live the educational service as a mission. This dedication and unselfishness contribute to characterising the school environment as a vital environment in which intellectual growth is harmonised with spiritual, religious, emotional and social growth.

Personalised accompanying

*giving
precedence
to dialogue
and
attentive
listening*

62. With the typical sensitivity of their formation, consecrated persons offer personalised accompanying through attentive listening and dialogue. They are, in fact, convinced that "education is a thing of the heart"[43] and that, consequently, an authentic formative process can only be initiated through a personal relationship.

*re-
awakening
the desire
for internal
liberation*

63. Every human being feels that he is internally oppressed by tendencies to evil, even when he flaunts limitless freedom. Consecrated men and women strive to reawaken in young people the desire for an internal liberation. This is a condition for undertaking the Christian journey that is directed towards the new life of the evangelical beatitudes. The evangelical view

---

[43] St JOHN BOSCO, *Circolare del 24 gennaio 1883,* in CERIA E. (*a cura di*), *Epistolario di S Giovanni Bosco,* SEI, Torino 1959, vol. IV, 209.

will allow young people to take an critical attitude towards consumerism and hedonism that have wormed their way, like the tare in the wheat, into the culture and way of life of vast areas of humanity.

Fully aware that all human values find their full accomplishment and their unity in Christ, consecrated persons explicitly represent the maternal care of the Church for the complete growth of the young people of our time, communicating the conviction that there can be no true liberation if there is no conversion of the heart.[44]

that is conversion of the heart

The dignity of woman and her vocation

64. The sensitivity of consecrated persons, so attentive to the need to develop the single-dual dimension of the human person in obedience to God's original plan (cf. *Gen* 2:18), can contribute to integrating differences in the educational endeavour to make maximum use of them and overcoming homologations and stereotypes. History testifies to the commitment of consecrated men and women in favour of women. Even today consecrated persons feel they have a duty to appreciate women in the field of education. In various parts of the world Catholic schools and numerous religious families are active in assuring that women are guaranteed access to education without any discrimination and that they can give their specific contribution to the good of the entire community. Everyone is aware of the contribution of women in favour of life and of the humanisation of culture,[45] their readiness to care for people and to rebuild the social tissue that has often been broken and torn by tension and hate. Many initiatives of solidarity, even among peoples at war, are born from that *female genius* that

The presence and action of women

---

[44] Cf. PAUL VI, Apostolic exhortation *Evangelii nuntiandi*, 8th December 1975, n. 36, *AAS* 68 (1976), 29
[45] Cf. JOHN PAUL II, Apostolic exhortation *Christifideles laici*, 30th December 1988, n. 51, *AAS* 81 (1989), 492-496.

promotes sensitivity for all human beings in all circumstances.[46] In this context consecrated women are called in a very special way to be, through their dedication lived in fullness and joy, *a sign of God's tender love towards the human race.*[47] The presence and appreciation of women is therefore essential for preparing a culture that really does place at its centre people, the search for the peaceful settlement of conflicts, unity in diversity, assistance and solidarity.

Intercultural outlook

Contribution of consecrated persons to intercultural dialogue

65. In today's complex society, schools are called to provide young generations with the elements necessary for developing an intercultural vision. Consecrated persons involved in education, who often belong to institutes that are spread throughout the world, are an expression of "multi-cultural and International communities, called to 'witness to the sense of communion among peoples, races and cultures' . . . where mutual knowledge, respect, esteem and enrichment are being experienced."[48] For this reason they can easily consider cultural differences as a richness and propose accessible paths of encounter and dialogue. This attitude is a precious contribution for true intercultural education, something that is made increasingly urgent by the considerable phenomenon of migration. The itinerary to be followed in educational communities involves passing from tolerance of the multicultural situation to welcome and a search for reasons for mutual understanding to intercultural dialogue, which leads to acknowledging the values and limits of every culture.

---

[46] Cf. JOHN PAUL II, Apostolic letter *Mulieris dignitatem,* 15th August 1988, n. 30, *AAS* 80 (1988), 1724-1727.
[47] Cf. JOHN PAUL II, Apostolic exhortation *Vita consecrata,* n. 57, *AAS* 88 (1996), 429.
[48] CONGREGATION FOR INSTITUTES OF CONSECRATED LIFE AND SOCIETIES OF APOSTOLIC LIFE, *Starting Afresh from Christ,* n. 29.

Intercultural education

66. From a Christian viewpoint, intercultural *Education* education is essentially based on the relational model *application* that is open to reciprocity. In the same way as happens *necessary* with people, cultures also develop through the typical dynamisms of dialogue and communion. "Dialogue between cultures emerges as an intrinsic demand of human nature itself, as well as of culture. It is dialogue which protects the distinctiveness of cultures as historical and creative expressions of the underlying unity of the human family, and which sustains understanding and communion between them. The notion of communion, which has its source in Christian revelation and finds its sublime prototype in the Triune God (cf. *Jn* 17:11, 21), never implies a dull uniformity or enforced homogenisation or assimilation; rather it expresses the convergence of a multiform variety, and is therefore a sign of richness and a promise of growth."[49]

Coexistence of differences

67. The intercultural prospective involves a change of paradigm at the pedagogical level. From the integration of differences one passes to a search for their coexistence. This is a model that is neither simple nor easily implemented. In the past, diversity between cultures was often a source of misunderstandings and conflicts; even today, in various parts of the world, we see the arrogant establishment of some cultures over others. No less dangerous is the tendency to homologation of cultures to models of the western world inspired by forms of radical individualism and a practically atheist concept of life.

---

[49] JOHN PAUL II, *Dialogue between Cultures for a Civilisation of Love and Peace,* Message for the Celebration of the World Day of Peace, 1st January 2001, n. 10, *AAS* 93 (2001), 239.

Commitment 68. Schools must question themselves about the
to seek the fundamental ethical trends that characterise the cultural
ethical experiences of a particular community. "Cultures, like the
foundations people who give rise to them, are marked by the 'mystery
of the of evil' at work in human history (cf. *1 Th* 2:7), and they
various too are in need of purification and salvation. The
cultures authenticity of each human culture, the soundness of its
underlying *ethos,* and hence the validity of its moral
bearings, can be measured to an extent by its commitment
to the human cause and by its capacity to promote human
dignity at every level and in every circumstance."[50]

In his speech to the members of the 50th General
Assembly of the United Nations Organisation, the
Pope underlined the fundamental communion between
peoples, observing that the various cultures are in
actual fact just different ways of dealing with the
question of the meaning of personal existence. In fact,
every culture is an attempt to reflect on the mystery of
the world and of man, a way of expressing the
transcendent dimension of human life. Seen this way,
difference, rather than being a threat, can become,
through respectful dialogue, a source of deep
understanding of the mystery of human existence.[51]

Sharing with the poor in solidarity

Preferential 69. The presence of consecrated persons in an
option for educational community concurs in perfecting the
the poor sensitivity of everyone to the poverty that still
torments young people, families and entire peoples.
This sensitivity can become a source of profound
changes in an evangelical sense, inducing a
transformation of the logics of excellence and
superiority into those of service, of *caring for others*
and forming a heart that is open to solidarity.

[50] *Ibid.,* n. 8, 238.
[51] Cf. JOHN PAUL II, *Insegnamenti,* XVIII/ 2, 1995, 730-744.

The preferential option for the poor leads to avoiding all forms of exclusion. Within the school there is often an educational plan that serves the more or less well-to-do social groups, while attention for the most needy definitively takes second place. In many cases social, economic or political circumstances leave no better alternative. This, however, must not mean the exclusion of a clear idea of the evangelical criteria or of trying to apply it at a personal and community level and within the scholastic institutions themselves.

Planning starting from the least

70. When the preferential option for the poorest is at the centre of the educational programme, the best resources and most qualified persons are initially placed at the service of the least, without in this way excluding those who have less difficulties and shortages. This is the meaning of evangelical inclusion, so distant from the logic of the world. The Church does, in fact, mean to offer its educational service *in the first place* to "those who are poor in the goods of this world or who are deprived of the assistance and affection of a family or who are strangers to the gift of Faith."[52] Unjust situations often make it difficult to implement this choice. Sometimes, however, it is Catholic educational institutions themselves that have strayed from such a preferential option, which characterised the beginnings of the majority of institutes of consecrated life devoted to teaching.

Poor young people at the centre of the education programme

This choice, typical of the consecrated life, should therefore be cultivated from the time of initial formation, so that it is not considered as reserved only for the most generous and courageous.

[52] SECOND VATICAN ECUMENICAL COUNCIL, Declaration on Catholic Education *Gravissimum educationis*, n. 9.

41

Identify situations of poverty 71. Following in the footsteps of the Good Shepherd, consecrated persons should identify among their pupils the various poverty situations that prevent the overall maturation of the person and marginalise him or her from social life, by investigating their causes. Among these, destitution occupies an undisputable place. It often brings with it the lack of a family and of health, social maladjustment, loss of human dignity, impossibility of access to culture and consequently a deep spiritual poverty. *Becoming the voice of the poor of the world* is a challenge assumed by the Church, and all Christians should do the same.[53] Due to their choices and their publicly professed commitment of a poor personal and community lifestyle of poverty, consecrated persons are more strongly sensitive to their duty to promote justice and solidarity in the environment in which they are active.

Giving voice to the poor

Considering the least 72. Access to education especially for the poor[54] is a commitment assumed at different levels by Catholic educational institutions. This requires arranging educational activity to suit the least, no matter what the social status of the pupils present in the scholastic institution. This involves, among other things, proposing the contents of the social doctrine of the Church through educational projects and requires checking the profile that the school foresees for its students. If a school listens to the poorest people and arranges itself to suit them, it will be able to interpret the subjects at the service of life, and avail of their contents in relation to the global growth of people.

---

[53] Cf. JOHN PAUL II, Apostolic letter *Tertio millennio adveniente,* 10th November 1994, n. 51, *AAS* 87 (1995), 36.
[54] See, for example, OFFICE INTERNATIONAL POUR L'ENSEIGNEMENT CATHOLIQUE (OIEC), *Déclaration de la XIVème Assemblée Générale,* Rome, 5th March 1994.

73. By listening to the poor, consecrated persons know *where* to commit themselves even within the sphere of non-formal education and how to bring the most underprivileged to have access to instruction. Acquaintance with countries where schools are reserved for the few or encounter serious difficulties in accomplishing their task could give rise in the educational communities of the more developed countries to initiatives of solidarity, among which twinning between classes or schools. The formative advantages would be great for everyone, especially for the pupils of the more developed countries. They would learn what is essential in life and they would be assisted in not following the cultural fashions induced by consumerism.

commitment in formal and non-formal education

74. The defence of children's rights is another particularly important challenge. The exploitation of children, in different, often aberrant, forms, is among the most disturbing aspects of our time. Consecrated persons involved in the educational mission have the inescapable duty to devote themselves to the protection and promotion of children's rights. The concrete contributions that they can make both as individuals and as an educational institution will probably be insufficient with respect to the needs, but not useless, inasmuch as aimed at making known the roots from which the abuses derive. Consecrated persons willingly unite their efforts to those of other civil and ecclesial organisations and persons of good will, to uphold the respect of human rights in for the good of everyone, starting from the most weak and helpless.

and in the defence of children's rights

75. The preferential option for the poor requires living a personal and community attitude of readiness to *give one's life* where necessary. It might therefore be

willing even to give their lives

43

necessary to leave perhaps even works of prestige which are no longer able to implement suitable formative processes and consequently leave no room for the characteristics of the consecrated life. In fact, "if a school is excellent as an academic institution, but does not bear witness to authentic values, then both good pedagogy and a concern for pastoral care make it obvious that renewal is called for."[55]

Consecrated persons are therefore called to check to see if, in their educational activity, they are mainly pursuing academic prestige rather than the human and Christian maturation of the young people; if they are favouring competition rather than solidarity; if they are involved in educating, together with the other members of the school community, persons who are free, responsible and *just* according to evangelical justice.

to the ends 76. Precisely because of their religious consecration,
of the earth consecrated persons are pre-eminently free to leave everything to go to preach the gospel even to the ends of the earth.[56] For them, even in the educational field, the announcement *"ad gentes"* of the Good News remains a priority. They are therefore aware of the fundamental role of Catholic schools in mission countries. In many cases, in fact, schools are the only possibility for the Church's presence, in others they are a privileged place of evangelising and humanising action, responsible both for the human and cultural development of the poorest people. It is important in this regard to consider the necessity of the participation of the educational charism between the religious families of the countries of ancient evangelisation and those born in mission territories,

---

[55] CONGREGATION FOR CATHOLIC EDUCATION, *The Religious Dimension of Education in a Catholic School*, n. 19.
[56] Cf. PAUL VI, Apostolic exhortation *Evangelii nuntiandi*, n. 69, *AAS* 68 (1976), 58.

which inspire them. In fact, "the older Institutes, many of which have been tested by the severest of hardships, which they have accepted courageously down the centuries can be enriched through dialogue and an exchange of gifts with the foundations appearing in our own days."[57] Such sharing is also transferred into the field of formation of consecrated persons, in sustaining new religious families and in cooperation between various institutes.

Culture of peace

77. The path to peace passes through justice. "Only in this way can we ensure a peaceful future for our world and remove the root causes of conflicts and wars: peace is the fruit of justice . . . a justice which is not content to apportion to each his own, but one which aims at creating conditions of *equal opportunity* among citizens, and therefore favouring those who, for reasons of social status or education or health, risk being left behind or being relegated to the lowest places in society, without possibility of deliverance."[58]

Peace through justice

Educating for peace starting from the heart

78. Awareness that education is the main road to peace is a fact shared by the international community. The various projects launched by international organisations for sensitising public opinion and governments are a clear sign of this.[59] Consecrated persons, witnesses of Christ, the Prince of Peace, grasp the urgency of placing education for peace among the primary objectives of their formative action offering

Peace-makers in their own environment

---

[57] JOHN PAUL II, Apostolic exhortation *Vita consecrata*, n. 62, AAS 88 (1996), 437.
[58] JOHN PAUL II, *Jubilee of Government Leaders, Members of Parliament and Politicians,* Rome, 4th November 2000, n. 2, AAS 93 (2001), 167.
[59] For example, the United Nations has promoted the *International Decade for a Culture of Peace and Non-violence,* (2000-2010).

their specific contribution to encourage in the hearts of the pupils the desire to become peacemakers. Wars in fact are born in the hearts of men and the defences of peace must be built in the hearts of men. By enhancing the educational process, consecrated persons undertake to excite attitudes of peace in the souls of the men of the third millennium. This "is not only the absence of conflict but requires a positive, dynamic, participatory process where dialogue is encouraged and conflicts are solved in a spirit of mutual understanding and co-operation."[60]

Consecrated persons cooperate in this undertaking with all men and women of goodwill sharing with them the effort and urgency to always seek new ways that are suited for an effective education that "has widened possibilities for strengthening a culture of peace."[61]

through the education to values 79. An effective education for peace involves preparing various levels of programmes and strategies. Among other things, it is a matter of proposing to the pupils an education to suitable values and attitudes for peacefully settling disputes in the respect of human dignity; of organising activities, even extracurricular ones such as sports and theatre that favour assimilating the values of loyalty and respect of rules; of assuring equality of access to education for women; of encouraging, when necessary, a review of curricula, including textbooks.[62]

Education is also called to transmit to students an awareness of their cultural roots and respect for other cultures. When this is achieved with solid ethical reference points, education leads to a realisation of the inherent limits in one's own culture and in that of others. At the same time, however, it emphasises a common

---

[60] THE UNITED NATIONS, *Résolution 53/243: Déclaration et Programme d'action sur une culture de la paix,* 6 october 1999.
[61] *Ibid.,* A, art. 1a; art. 4.
[62] Cf. *Ibid.,* B, art. 9.

inheritance of values to the entire human race. In this way *"education has a particular role to play in building a more united and peaceful world.* It can help to affirm that integral humanism, open to life's ethical and religious dimension, which appreciates the importance of understanding and showing esteem for other cultures and the spiritual values present in them."[63]

Educating for coexistence

80. As a result of the negative effects of uncontrolled economic and cultural globalisation, responsible participation in the life of the community at local, national and world levels acquires increasing importance at the beginning of the third millennium. This participation presupposes the realisation of the causes of the phenomena that threaten the coexistence of people and of human life itself. As with every realisation, this too finds in education, and in particular in schools, fertile ground for its development. Thus a new and difficult task takes shape: educate to have active and responsible citizens. The words of the Pope are enlightening in this regard: "promoting the right to peace ensures respect for all other rights, since it encourages the building of a society in which structures of power give way to structures of cooperation, with a view to the common good."[64] In this respect, consecrated persons can offer the sign of a responsible brotherhood, living in communities in which "each member has a sense of co-responsibility for the faithfulness of the others; each one contributes to a serene climate of sharing life, of understanding, and of mutual help."[65]

Educating for active and responsible citizens

---

[63] JOHN PAUL II, *Dialogue between Cultures for a Civilisation of Love and Peace,* Message for the Celebration of the World Day of Peace, 1st January 2001, n. 20, *AAS* 93 (2001), 245.
[64] JOHN PAUL II, *Respect for Human Rights: the Secret of True Peace,* Message for the Celebration of the World Day of Peace, 1st January 1999, n. 11, *AAS* 91 (1999), 385.
[65] CONGREGATION FOR INSTITUTES OF CONSECRATED LIFE AND SOCIETIES OF APOSTOLIC LIFE, *Fraternal Life in Community,* 2nd February 1994, n.57, in *Enchiridion Vaticanum,* vol. 14, 265.

CONCLUSION

81. The reflections proposed clearly indicate that the presence of consecrated persons in the world of education is a prophetic choice.[66]

The Synod on the consecrated life exhorts to assume with renewed dedication the educational mission in all levels of schools, universities and institutions of higher learning.[67] The invitation to continue the itinerary begun by those who have already offered a significant contribution to the educational mission of the Church lies within the bounds of the fidelity to their original charism: "because of their special consecration, their particular experience of the gifts of the Spirit, their constant listening to the Word of God, their practice of discernment, their rich heritage of pedagogical traditions built up since the establishment of their Institute, and their profound grasp of spiritual truth (cf. *Ef* 1:17), consecrated persons are able to be especially effective in educational activities and to offer a specific contribution to the work of other educators."[68]

Starting afresh from Christ

82. In the dimension of ecclesial communion, there is a growing awareness in every consecrated person of the great cultural and pedagogical wealth that derives from sharing a common educational mission, even in the specificity of the various ministries and charisms. It is a matter of discovering and renewing an awareness of one's own identity, finding again the inspiring nucleuses of a skilled educational

---

[66] Cf. CONGREGATION FOR CATHOLIC EDUCATION, *The Catholic School on the Threshold of the Third Millennium*, n. 21.
[67] Cf. JOHN PAUL II, Apostolic exhortation *Vita consecrata*, n. 97, *AAS* 88 (1996), 473.
[68] *Ibid.*, n. 96, 472.

professionalism to be rediscovered as a way of being that represents an authentic vocation. The root of this renewed awareness is Christ. Consecrated persons working in schools must start from him to find again the motivating source of their mission. Starting afresh from Christ means contemplating his face, pausing at length with him in prayer to then be able to show him to others. It is what the Church is called to accomplish at the beginning of the new millennium, conscious that only faith can enter the mystery of that face.[69] Starting again from Christ is, therefore, also for consecrated men and women, starting afresh from faith nourished by the sacraments and supported by a hope that does not fail: "I am with you always" (*Mt* 28:20). Encouraged by this hope, consecrated persons are called to revive their educational passion living it in school communities as a testimony of encounter between different vocations and between generations.

The task of teaching to live, discovering the deepest meaning of life and of transcendence, to mutually interact with others, to love creation, to think freely and critically, to find fulfilment in work, to plan the future, in one word to *be,* demands a new love of consecrated persons for educational and cultural commitment in schools. *in a renewed commitment*

83. By allowing themselves to be transformed by the Spirit and living in a state of permanent formation, consecrated men and women become able to extend their horizons and understand the profound causes of events.[70] Permanent formation also becomes the key to understanding the educational mission in schools and for carrying it out in a way that is close to a reality that is so changeable and at the same time in need of *and living in a state of permanent formation*

[69] Cf. JOHN PAUL II, Apostolic letter *Novo millennio ineunte*, n. 19, *AAS* 93 (2001), 278-279.
[70] Cf. JOHN PAUL II, Apostolic exhortation *Vita consecrata*, n. 98, *AAS* 88 (1996), 474.

responsible, timely and prophetic intervention. The cultural study that consecrated persons are called to cultivate for improving their professionalism in the subjects for which they are responsible, or in the administrative or management service, is a duty of justice, which cannot be shirked.

Participation in the life of the universal and particular Church involves demonstrating the bonds of communion and appreciating the directions of the Magisterium, especially with regard to such matters as life, the family, the issue of women, social justice, peace, ecumenism, inter-religious dialogue. In the climate of modern pluralism, the Magisterium of the Church is the voice of authority that interprets phenomena in the light of the Gospel.

Thanks-giving for the important and noble task

84. The Congregation for Catholic Education wishes to conclude these reflections with sincere gratitude to all the consecrated persons who work in the field of school education. While aware of the complexity and often of the difficulties of their task, it wishes to underline the value of the *noble* educational service aimed at giving reasons for life and hope to the new generations, through critically processed knowledge and culture, on the basis of a concept of the person and of life inspired by the evangelical values.

Every school and every place of non formal education can become a centre of a greater network which, from the smallest village to the most complex metropolis, wraps the world in hope. It is in education, in fact, that the promise of a more human future and a more harmonious society lies.

No difficulty should remove consecrated men and women from schools and from education in general, when the conviction of being called to bring the Good News of the Kingdom of God to the poor and small is so deep and vital. Modern difficulties and confusion, together with the new prospects that are appearing at the dawn of the third millennium, are a strong reminder to pass one's life in educating the new generations to become bearers of a culture of communion that may reach every people and every person. The main motive and, at the same time, the goal of the commitment of every consecrated person, is to light and trim the lamp of faith of the new generations, the "morning watchmen (cf. *Is* 21:11-12) at the dawn of the new millennium."[71]

The Holy Father, during the Audience granted to the undersigned Prefect, approved this document and authorised its publication.

Rome, 28th October 2002, thirty-seventh anniversary of the promulgation of the statement *Gravissimum educationis* of the Second Vatican Council.

Zenon Card. GROCHOLEWSKI
Prefect

✠ Joseph PITTAU, S.J.
Secretary

---

[71] JOHN PAUL II, Apostolic letter *Novo millennio ineunte*, n. 9, AAS 93 (2001), 272.